Angel

Now That's What I Call Christmas

A humorous retelling of the Nativity story,
told through the eyes of a bunch of angels.

Dave is a freelance author and speaker, and is
available for workshops, seminars
and speaking engagements.

www.davehopwood.com

© 2018 Dave Hopwood.

For Amy

Thanks for all your encouragement
and for the idea of doing this book

x x x x

Characters

4 Angels:

      – Michael

      – Gabriel

      – Smith

      – Jones

Zechariah – a priest

Shepherd 1

Shepherd 2

Melchior – a wise man

6 Marys

      – the 6th Mary is Jesus's mum

Mary's mum

Joseph – a carpenter/builder, engaged to Mary

A few sheep

One

Three angels wander into a conference room somewhere in heaven. Smith and Jones are well-meaning if somewhat flippant and action-loving, Gabriel is earnest, keen and a little more experienced. He hovers in the background as Smith and Jones banter.

Smith – So did you see *Heaven's Got Talent* last night? I can't believe that guy with the talking donkey won.

Jones – I voted for the bloke who managed to cram a million animals into that boat the size of the Tardis.

Smith – You going to the Inter-angelic FA Cup Final?

Jones – What? Cherubim Wednesday verses Seraphim Wanderers? You're kidding. I'm a Messengers fan myself.

Smith – Look lively, big Mike's here!

The three form a straggly line as Michael strides in, tall, shiny and very much the man in charge. He walks along the line sighing and tutting as he inspects the ragged trio. When he reaches the far end he magically produces a clipboard.

Michael – Right you lot, this is a tough assignment. We have to get this right. There's never been a mission like this in all of history. Angel Smith...

Smith – Sir?

Michael – Don't kill anyone, all right?

Smith – Why not?

Michael – Because it's not that kind of assignment.

Smith – Oh!

Michael – You hear me? No killing!

Smith – Not even a little bit?

Michael – Not even a little bit.

Smith – But I was allowed to kill people in Egypt.

Michael – This is not Egypt. Times have changed. You can't go around wiping out every firstborn child.

Jones raises a finger – Sir?

Michael – Angel Jones?

Jones – What about every second-born child?

Michael – No!

Smith – Every third-born?

Michael – No!

Jones – Every fourth-born?

Michael – No! This mission is about protecting life. There are two firstborn sons and they need to make it through.

Smith – Well… can we kill their enemies?

Michael – No!

Jones – Can we bash them about a bit?

Michael – No!

Smith – Can we flick their ears and jab them in the bottom?

Michael – Listen. There will be no flicking or jabbing. You just have to deliver a message.

Jones – A message!! Is that it?

Michael – Yep. To a bunch of smelly shepherds… I mean to a collective of aroma-specific animal carers. Gabriel, you're in charge of that particular mission. I'll give you a list of all the other key engagements with humans that you need to undertake as well.

Smith – Do we have to engage with so many humans? They have weird habits and seem to think the universe revolves around them. Plus they scratch and sweat and sneeze and spit! And they stare for hours at little slabs of glass and plastic. I mean - what's going on there?!

Jones – Yea, and what's with that thing where they put little paper tubes in their mouth and - get this - set fire to them!

Smith – And they eat Marmite! What's that all about!?

Jones – For decades I never actually believed in human beings. I thought they didn't exist. They sounded so mad!

Michael – Don't worry. Gabriel's doing most of the missions alone.

Gabriel – What!!

Michael – You'll do fine. You just need to visit John's dad, Jesus's mum, Jesus's dad, and a few wise men. Make sure you don't step in any camel droppings though, I don't know what they feed those creatures on, but it stains. Not to mention the smell. And don't hang around too long at the face end either - those things can spit like a fire hose. Now, here are the details.

Michael hands a long slip of paper to Gabriel.

Smith – How about King Herod?

Michael – No. There are no messages for King Herod.

Smith – Yea, but can we kill him?

Michael – No!

Smith – But it's not fair. He's horrible. How about we put a bat up his trousers?

Jones – Yea - a vampire bat.

Michael – Go and deliver those messages - and don't hurt anyone on the way.

Smith – We could put ants in his pants.

Jones – Or llamas in his pyjamas?

Smith – Sticky Toffee Pudding in his socks?

Jones – Superglue in his toothpaste?

Smith – Cling film on his toilet?

Jones – Stilton cheese in his underarm roll-on?

Gabriel – Look you two this is getting stupid. We should listen to Michael, stop messing about and be serious.

Michael – Thank you Gabriel. Well said.

Smith – Yes, sorry, you're absolutely right. We should be serious about this. We should seriously stuff fish fingers up his nose.

Michael – I'm warning you - you'll be grounded if you don't be quiet. Now off you go.

Michael leaves.

Smith – It's so unfair - it's not like the old days.

Jones – Yea, they never let me play the angel of death anymore. Still, we could scare them shepherds when we first appear, make it look like we're about to nuke them.

Smith – Good idea! Zap!

He jabs his fingers at the air.

Jones – Fire and brimstone!

Smith puts on a scary voice – Death to shepherds!!!

Angels Smith and Jones break into song together at this point –
'Hark the herald angels sing,
You're gonna die you naughty things!
Angels from the realms of glory,
Things will soon get really gory!!'

Smith – Can't wait till Armageddon.

Jones – Yea, payback time!

Smith – I'm in charge of bringing plague and pestilence.

Jones – Oh that's not fair, I wanted to do that!

Smith – Tough. You can do fire and brimstone.

Jones – Oh! That's boring. How about we trade? I'll swap you two bowls of wrath, and the big sharp sickle of death.

Smith – I am not trading.

Jones – I'll throw in the four horsemen of the apocalypse?

Gabriel – Ooh that's tempting.

Jones – Exactly! Come on.

Smith – Nope.

Gabriel – I could swap you floods, famine and the winepress of total annihilation?

Jones – Hey! You can't - I'm the one doing the trade. How about the seven trumpets of doom?

Michael sticks his head back in at this point.

Michael – Oy! Are you lot still here? Stop bickering – you've got important messages to deliver. Gabriel, come with me, I want to talk you through that list I gave you. Walk with me, I'll explain as we go.

Gabriel hurries off with Michael. Smith and Jones pull faces at each other, then produce pea shooters and start firing peas at one another.

Two

Michael and Gabriel stroll the corridors of heaven.

Michael – Gabriel, this is a big assignment you know.

Gabriel – Really?

Michael – Yes, really. Huge! Massive. Colossal.

Gabriel – Is it helping an old man cross the road?

Michael – No.

Gabriel – Helping a young man cross the road?

Michael – Nope.

Gabriel – Helping a cat cross the road?

Michael – NO!

Gabriel – A squirrel?

Michael – It's much bigger than that.

Gabriel – Ooh! I know! Helping an old lady find a parking space.

Michael – No.

Gabriel – Helping a squirrel find a parking space?

Michael – Listen! Just listen. You need to find someone. The name's on that list I gave you.

Gabriel – Oh a missing person?

Michael – Not exactly.

Gabriel – A missing squirrel?

Michael – Stop it with the squirrels now, Gabriel. This is the start of the biggest assignment in history. Now listen very carefully, it may not be straightforward…

Three

The priest Zechariah makes his way carefully through the temple.

Gabriel – Er... excuse me…

Zechariah – Aghhhhh!!! What are you doing in here? You can't be in here!

Gabriel – Are you er…

He checks his bit of paper.

Gabriel – Zechariah by any chance?

Zechariah – We're all gonna die!!

Gabriel – Who is?

Zechariah – You! Me! You can't just saunter in here like this!

Gabriel – I didn't saunter. I never saunter!

Zechariah – This is terrible. I'm too young to die.

Gabriel – Well you're not that young. That's why I'm here.

Zechariah – What?

Gabriel – I've got a message for you.

Zechariah – Well couldn't it wait?

Gabriel – No. This is the appointed time.

Zechariah – Appointed or not you'll get us both killed. Only the chosen priests can come in here and then only twice a year. We can't have any Tom, Dick or Harry shilly-shallying around in here.

Gabriel – I'm not Tom, Dick or Harry. And I've never shilly-shallied in my life, I'll have you know. So where is he?

Zechariah – Who?

Gabriel – This chosen priest chap?

Zechariah – It's me! It's my turn, it doesn't come around that often and you've just ruined it. My life's over.

Gabriel – I doubt it!

Zechariah – It is! We can't just meander into the glory of God any time we want. It can be fatal.

Gabriel – Once again… I never meander. And this whole thing is *about* the glory of God. Now listen, Zechariah, don't panic, but you and Elizabeth are going to have a baby.

Zechariah – What? Have you seen how old we are?

Gabriel – A minute ago you were too young to die. Now shush. This boy will bring joy to lots of people, and he will prepare folks for the arrival of God among them. He'll be like Elijah and will soften the hearts of many. Now, don't let him have a drink of wine, or beer, or spirits...

Zechariah – Shandy?

Gabriel – Shandy?

Zechariah – Yes, you know you can buy those cans in the corner shop with barely any kick in them at all.

Gabriel – No! No shandy! He'll be filled with another spirit all his life, the spirit of God. And he'll turn many rebels back to God. Got it?

Zechariah – Yes, I think so... it's a bit of a shock but... I'll go straight away. As soon as I've finished here.

Gabriel – Go where? Where are you going?

Zechariah – The adoption agency...

Gabriel – No, no, no! You're not listening. You're gonna have a baby. You and Elizabeth. Well mostly Elizabeth. Your own baby. You know, food cravings and Braxton hicks and morning sickness.

Zechariah – But you're not serious? We're too old. That would be... well... a little thing we might call - *impossible*. I think I'm gonna need some proof here!

Gabriel – Proof? No. But it'll happen. Trust me. I know about these things. I'm an angel!

Zechariah – An angel! So that's how you got in. What a relief, I'm not gonna die.

Gabriel – NO! You're gonna have a baby. But seeing as you doubt me I'll give you a sign, you'll be shtum…

Zechariah – Schtum??

Gabriel – Yea, silent. Buttoned up. Zipped. Till John's born.

Zechariah – Who's John?

Gabriel – Your baby!

Zechariah – But…

Gabriel – Now be quiet.

And he so he is, for nine months. Much as Zechariah does his best to shout, whisper, mutter and mumble… nothing comes out. He has to mime the message to his wife Elizabeth about her having a baby. And then *she* is speechless for a while. Till she recovers from the shock. After that they go to bed, and she wakes up pregnant!

Four

Gabriel walks the streets looking lost. He mutters to himself, shaking his head. This is a different kind of job. He feels the weight of it. The importance. He sighs a lot and pats his pockets repeatedly as he walks.

Gabriel – I can't believe it. I just can't. I cannot believe it. I've lost it. I've lost the house number. The one thing I needed to not lose. What did Michael say? 'Don't lose the house number.' What have I done? Lost the house number. How could I do it? I can't go back, they'll all laugh at me. I'll just have to look around till I find the right address. It's this street, I'm fairly sure. She's in this road somewhere.

He stops and looks at a door, one of many in a terrace of houses. He makes a fist, puffs out his cheeks and knocks. Very quietly. No one hears, so he has to knock again, louder this time. He panics as he hears footsteps approaching inside the house. He looks for somewhere to hide, there is nowhere. He's still panicking when the door opens.

Woman – Yes?

Gabriel – Oh! Er… well… is your name Mary… by any chance?

Woman – Yea.

Gabriel – Brilliant! First time! I mean, what I mean to say is, I have a message for you. Mary don't be afraid, I have good news for you, you're going to have a baby.

Mary – I know.

Gabriel – What?

Mary – I know, I found out just now!

She smiles and holds up a pregnancy tester.

Mary – How did you know about it?

Gabriel – Oh! Sorry – wrong one. Oops!

Mary – What?

Gabriel – Sorry! Got to fly! I mean go.

Gabriel hurries off and looks for another door to try. Mary looks perplexed as she closes her front door. Gabriel waits till she's gone then knocks at another house three doors further down the street.

A voice calls from inside the house.

Voice – Yes?

Gabriel – Is your name Mary?

Voice from inside – Yes. What is it?

Gabriel – Great! You're going to have a …

Mary opens the door, she is heavily pregnant.

Gabriel – Never mind.

She closes the door and Gabriel walks away, deflated. He crosses the street. Recites a rhyme as he points at one house after another.

Gabriel – 'Hark the herald angels sing, glory to the new-born…' that'll do. I'll try that one.

Gabriel knocks again. The door opens, a young woman stands there, hands on her hips.

Gabriel – Is your name Mary?

Woman – It might be - who are you?

Gabriel – I have good news.

Woman – Are you selling something?

Gabriel – No. I've got good news.

Woman – That's what they all say. I don't want it.

Gabriel – But…

Woman – I don't want it.

She slams the door. Gabriel sighs and steps to the next house. He knocks again. He leaps back as the door opens quickly.

Woman – Hello?

Gabriel – You don't happen to be called Mary… do you? I'll even accept it as a middle name?

Woman – Yes! It *is* my middle name actually!

Gabriel – Great! That's good enough for me.

Mary – And my first name!

Gabriel – What?

Mary – My parents liked it so much they called me it twice. Mary Mary. Unusual, eh?

Gabriel – Er… yes…

Mary – My brother's called Mary too!

Gabriel – Right… look I'm very busy, sorry I've got to go. Nice to meet you.

Mary – But what did you want?

Gabriel starts to hurry away. He calls back to her.

Gabriel – Nothing! Never mind.

He leans against a nearby wall and wipes his brow.

Gabriel – Maybe I should just go back to Michael and ask him for the house number.

A young woman walks past and stops.

Woman – Are you looking for someone called Mary?

Gabriel – How did you know?

Woman – Word travels round here. I'm Mary. What do you want?

Gabriel – Oh brilliant! Thanks! I was just about to give up. Listen, I've got great news for you. God has smiled on you, you're going to be a mother.

Mary – One day, yes.

Gabriel – No. Soon.

Mary – Yes. Soon.

Gabriel – In nine months.

Mary laughs – I don't think so.

Gabriel – Yes Mary.

Mary – No… whatever your name is. And if this is some kind of chat-up line it's the worst one I've ever heard. Now go away.

The woman tuts, rolls her eyes and walks off.

Gabriel – I give up. Is everyone called Mary round here?

A woman walks past with a couple of full shopping bags. She stops and looks him up and down.

Woman – You look tired, would you like a drink? I've got some bottles of water.

Gabriel – Thanks. I'm worn out.

She smiles and hands him a small bottle from her shopping.

Woman – Are you looking for someone? They said a strange man was wandering round.

Gabriel – Yes, but… I'm not strange, and I'm not a man.

She looks him up and down.

Woman – Whatever you say.

A voice calls from a nearby house – Mary!

They look round, a woman is leaning out of a downstairs window.

Woman – Hang on mum, we've got a visitor.

She looks at Gabriel.

Woman – Sorry, I've got to go. We're planning the wedding. It's gonna be a big do. I mean… Joseph hasn't actually asked me to marry him yet, but you know what men are like… even if you're not one…

Looks him up and down again.

Gabriel – Yes well… Thanks for the drink.

Mary starts to leave.

Gabriel – Wait a minute - did… did that woman just call you Mary?

Mary – Yes. It's because - believe it or not - that's my name!

Gabriel – And did you say wedding?

Mary – Shh! We're keeping it quiet for now… me and mum have got it all mapped out though. No loose ends, no surprises, all nice and tidy. Nothing unexpected.

Gabriel – Then I'd better apologise now.

Mary – What d'you mean?

Gabriel – You know that bit about *no surprises*?

Mary – Yes…

Gabriel – Well you'd better sit down.

Mary – Why?

Gabriel – You haven't been feeling queasy have you? In the mornings?

Mary – No. I haven't… but I'm starting to now. What are you talking about?

Gabriel – D'you like babies?

Mary – Why? Have I won one or something?

Gabriel – Look, I know you've got other things on your mind, and I've got a hunch this is going to freak you out. But God has a plan - and he needs your help.

Mary – God? Are you mad?

Gabriel – You do believe in God, don't you?

Mary – Yes.

Gabriel – Well, he believes in you. And you may not be expecting this right now - but he's about to give you the best present anybody ever had.

Mary – Not a long weekend in New York?

Gabriel – No.

Mary – A trip to Disneyland?

Gabriel – No. A baby. You're pregnant.

Mary laughs.

Mary – I don't think so.

Gabriel – Yep.

Gabriel pulls out a crumpled sheet of paper and straightens it out so he can read the message on it. He takes a deep breath.

Gabriel – Nine months from now you'll have a baby, and this one won't just change your world he'll change everyone's. He'll be different, and the world will be different because of him.

Mary stares at him, mouth open.

Gabriel – I don't want to... you know - blind you with the science of it all - but the planet's in trouble right? Well, right there...

He points at her stomach. She looks down.

Gabriel – That's the solution.

Mary – Well, I don't want to blind you with the science - but there's no way that - right there…

Mary points dramatically at her own stomach.

Mary – There's a baby, know what I mean…

She gives a forced smile and an elaborate wink.

Gabriel – Trust me, I'm not a doctor, but there's a baby in there. God knows you Mary - you'll be fine.

Mary – Really…. but… really? How… I mean… I… you know… it can't be… I mean, how…

She stares at him, looking aghast.

Mary – Maybe it's another woman called Mary.

Gabriel – Trust me - I've tried all the others.

Mary – But… I haven't… done… you know - the biology bit… the science… it's… it's impossible…

Gabriel – Nothing's impossible with God, Mary.

She thinks for a minute.

Mary – Really? Well… if you say so.

Gabriel – I do. Now don't worry, God is on your side and he thinks you're brilliant and perfect for the job…

Mary – Can I have a girl?

Gabriel – What?

Mary – Can I have a girl?

Gabriel – No! There's a plan.

Mary – Twins then? One of each?

Gabriel – No! It doesn't work like that. You're going to have a baby boy and call him Jesus. Look, I'd better go cause you're about to get a call. It's from your cousin - Liz, she's er…

Gabriel pats his stomach.

Gabriel – ….as well! Gotta fly.

He leaves. Mary's phone rings. Mary looks amazed and answers it.

Mary – Hello? Liz? How are you? What? Are you sure? I mean… what exactly do you mean when you say - 'you're pregnant'?

Mary walks off, listening on her phone.

Five

A few days pass and Joseph hears of Mary's pregnancy. He is not happy, to put it mildly. In those days, in their culture, this was a deeply shocking situation. But Joseph doesn't want to make a fuss so he decides to quietly call off the wedding. Then Gabriel sneaks into his bedroom one night.

Gabriel, grabbing his foot – Ow! Who left that chisel on the floor just there? That's gonna smart for days now! And oh great, he's asleep. I guess I could wake him up. Or maybe I'd better sneak into his dream instead. Hope it's not a scary violent one. Now how did they do it in that movie *Inception*? Hmm. Can't remember. Oh well. I'll just slide under his pillow and tunnel through his ear. Here goes. Ow! That's a squee-e-e-eze! Ouch! Right, I'm in. Now… what's that noise? Yikes! A roaring lion - coming right at me! Where's Joe? Oh! Inside the lion's mouth!? This is a weird dream. Suppose I'd better let the lion bite me… ulp! Ah there you are. Hi Joe.

Joseph – Who are you? And why are we in this lion's mouth?

Gabriel – It's a dream. Maybe it means something. Are you scared of lions?

Joseph – No, but I don't like pussycats.

Gabriel – There you go then. Now. Listen to me, it's about Mary.

Joseph – Mary? What about Mary?

Gabriel – This baby she's having…

Joseph – How d'you know about that?

Gabriel – It was me.

Joseph – What!!! You! What are you saying? You mean you're the fa…

Gabriel – No, no, no! I'm an angel.

Joseph – An angel? In a lion's mouth?

Gabriel – Well Jonah got swallowed by a whale. And Balaam had a talking donkey. What do you expect? Now, we haven't got much time, this lion's stomach is rumbling, he may well swallow us before too long. So on the subject of Mary - you've got to marry her.

Joseph – No way! I'll lose everything. My reputation. My friends. My standing in the community. My membership of the Round Table.

Gabriel – I don't care.

Joseph – What?

Gabriel – There more important things at stake. Would you rather have a Round Table lapel badge, or be the father of the boy who's going to save the world?

Joseph – Hmm. Is there a third option?

Gabriel – Don't be daft.

Joseph – Okay. I want to do the right thing. But I don't get it. Who's the father? I swear it's not me.

Gabriel – We know that. Look, you'd better sit down.

Joseph – I am sitting down, in a pool of lion's saliva.

Gabriel – Oh yea, I'll make this quick then. The baby inside Mary was conceived by God's Holy Spirit. There is no earthly father. Mary has done nothing wrong, in fact she's done everything right. I'll admit it took me a while to find her, but that was my fault. My desk is very untidy. I keep meaning to get a system…

Joseph – What?

Gabriel – Never mind about that. This baby of hers, this baby of yours, will be the Saviour of the world. Yes – seriously! Now are you on board? It won't be easy. It'll be no walk in the park, or a dream in a lion's mouth. But we have every faith in you Joe, you're a good, kind, courageous man. D'you want the job?

Joseph – I love Mary.

Gabriel – Good. Then show it. Stick by her and look after her baby. Now come on. Let's get out of this glob of lion's spittle.

Joseph – Is there an easy way to do that?

Gabriel – Yea!

Gabriel smiles and snaps his fingers, expecting to just disappear, but nothing happens. He snaps his fingers again, still nothing happens. He looks at Joseph, horrified, and snaps his fingers a third time.

Gabriel – I think I need new batteries in my fingers!

Joseph – Oh great.

Gabriel – Quick! Jump out!

The lion roars loudly, so Joseph and Gabriel look terrified, leap forwards and run off to the sound of more roaring.

Six

Angels Smith, Jones and Gabriel make their way from heaven to earth.

Smith – Are you sure we can't just nuke a couple of them? There are loads down there. No one'll notice.

Gabriel – No! You heard the plan. We turn the brightness up, swoop on down, put on a light show so humongous that it looks like a sky full of angels, and I tell them about the baby.

Smith – Couldn't we just have brought a sky full of angels?

Gabriel – Cutbacks. But we've got the high energy, low emission bulbs so we'll be fine.

Jones – It might get their attention if we nuke a couple of them.

Gabriel – This'll get their attention! They'll be scared enough as it is when they see us in the sky.

Smith – Can we sing something then?

Gabriel – What?

Smith – You know a couple of big stadium numbers. *Living on a Prayer* or something?

Gabriel – We don't need to! Just turn up the brightness to 11 and hang about near me.

Jones – I bet when they tell this story in the future everyone'll say we sang. I bet you anything.

Gabriel – There is nothing in the brief about singing! No killing and no singing. Got it?

Jones – It was hardly worth getting out of bed.

Smith – I might just hum something. You know, quietly.

Gabriel – No! No, no, no! N - O. Just let *me* do the talking. Now come on.

They fly down and light up the sky. The two shepherds in the field below see them and look terrified.

Shepherds – Yikes!! Help!! Run!!!

Gabriel – No need. We come in peace! I said... oh look at that... they're running away. Come back! Quick, we'd better get after them.

The angels swoop a little lower, while the shepherds duck behind some sheep.

Gabriel – We can see you there! Come out. There's no need to be afraid. We've got good news.

The sheep make a lot of noise with their baa-ing.

Gabriel – Can we turn the volume on the sheep down? Jones, can you take care of that?

Jones snaps his fingers and the sheep open their mouths but no sound comes out. The sheep look confused as they mime at each other.

Gabriel – Now, listen you lot down there, it's okay. It's safe, we've come to bring you good news. Come on, come out and say hello. Ah there you are. Now listen, your Saviour has been born - tonight - right down there in Bethlehem.

Shepherd 1 – Really?

Gabriel – Really.

Shepherd 2 – Really?

Gabriel – YES! REALLY!

Shepherd 1 – You're not kidding? This is not a trick? You're not going to nuke us?

Gabriel – Of course not. We bring you good news of great joy! Be happy! Go find the baby.

Shepherd 2 – But... there might be lots of babies down there...

Gabriel – Ooh yes, I forgot, thanks for reminding me. That's a vital bit. Well done for prompting me. You'll find him in an animal trough wrapped up in bits of cloth. Strips of linen, you know, that sort of thing.

Shepherd 1 – Now you are kidding. A new baby - the Saviour - in an animal trough? You're having a laugh.

Gabriel – No. That's how you'll know. He's easy to find, you won't have to go into some posh place smelling terrible. You'll be right at home there, among the animals. It's perfect. A king for the people. Go for it! Quick!

Shepherd 2 – Are you saying we smell bad?

Angels – Hurry! And when you've found him spread the good news. Come on Smith and Jones, help me out here!

Smith – What? Can we sing now?

Gabriel – No! The announcement we learnt, remember?

Smith – Oh right. Yea. Can you count us in? After three?

Gabriel – No, just get on with it.

All the angels announce – 'Glory to God in the highest and on earth peace amongst his people. Glory to God in the highest and on earth peace amongst his people.'

The shepherds look amazed and start making their way down the hill.

Jones – I thought we were going to say it three times. We practiced three times. You only did two!

Gabriel – Two's enough! Look they've got the message. Oh and you can turn the sheep back on now, Jones.

Jones snaps his fingers and the air is filled with bleating, so loud that it makes the sheep jump. The angels watch the shepherds run towards the town. Angel Smith shouts down to them.

Smith – Oy! Watch out down there, you're about to step in a huge big… oh! Never mind.

The angels head for home.

Gabriel – And you can turn the brightness down now too Jones. You're like a Christmas tree there!

Jones snaps his fingers again.

Gabriel – Oh and Smith, were you humming?

Smith – When?

Gabriel – When I was talking to the shepherds. Were you humming behind me?

Smith – Nope.

Gabriel – Are you sure? I could have sworn I heard a bit of that Robbie Williams song *Angels* coming from behind me.

Smith – Doubt it. It hasn't been written yet.

Gabriel – Hmm... all right. Come on, let's go and report back.

Jones – Can we kill anyone on the way?

Gabriel – No!

They turn and head back for heaven.

Smith – Ooh and watch out where you're treading Jones, there's that huge big... oh! Never mind.

They wander off, Jones shaking his foot as he goes, and looking rather unhappy.

Seven

Some time later (there are lots of theories about the timing of this bit of the story that frankly don't fit into a comedy retelling) Gabriel sneaks into the bedroom of three wise men.

Gabriel – Er… chaps? Lads? You three… wise blokes… hello? Are you asleep?

The wise men lie there snoring.

Gabriel – Right. I'll take that as a yes. I guess I'd better do that breaking into dreams bit again. I'll just sneak under this guy's pillow and squeeze in through his ear. Here I go… ugh, what's this waxy bit here?

Melchior – Ow! What's going on? Who are you? Why are you waking me up?

Gabriel – I haven't woken you up. This is a dream, mate. Now are you Gaspar?

Melchior – No - I'm Melchior.

Gabriel – Oh good, just as well, Gaspar always makes me think of that friendly ghost.

Melchior – What friendly ghost?

Gabriel – Casper. Oh, don't worry. You'd only know if you're outside of time. I'm a good twenty thousand years old. You should see the number of candles on my last birthday cake!

We needed scaffolding to support the thing! We had the celestial fire department on standby. Anyway, you know that king you went to see?

Melchior – Oh the baby? He's beautiful!

Gabriel – No the other one. The one who wasn't beautiful. The one who smelt bad. The one you *weren't* supposed to go and see.

Melchior – Shhhh! We don't want anyone to know we botched it up.

Gabriel – Too late - it's gone down in history mate.

Melchior – Well it was Balthasar's fault. I wanted to go and get a map from the tourist office.

Gabriel – Whatever. Anyway, don't go and see the king again.

Melchior – The little baby? Ohhh…

Gabriel – No! The big smelly horrible king. What's his name? Hagrid?

Melchior – Herod.

Gabriel – That's the one. Avoid him like the plague. In fact he does have the plague. And it won't be long before his guts go all wormy, he itches all over, his bottom bits turn putrid and he goes a bit bonkers.

Melchior – Will he get better?

Gabriel – Not a chance. He'll run out of breath before long, which of course is what gets most people in the end. But in the meantime stay away from Team Hagrid…

Melchior – You mean Herod…

Gabriel – Yea, him too. Don't have tea and cake or curry and chips or pie and mash or anything with anything with him okay?

Melchior – In case we catch something?

Gabriel – In case he catches you, and hangs you upside-down by your earlobes till you tell him where the new baby is, okay? Hagrid's a nasty case of doggy-dos. No other word for him. He's insanely jealous and isn't happy about the news of a new king in town. So just pack up your gold and your myrrh and your Frankenstein and go home.

Melchior – But we bought those things for the baby. Sort of like Christening presents.

Gabriel – Myrrh? Are you kidding?

Melchior – They're symbolic. Gold because he's a king, frankincense because he's the son of God and myrrh because…

Gabriel – Yea?

Melchior – Well…

Gabriel – Yea?

Melchior – You know - for… dead bodies.

Gabriel – Oh of course, perfect. Just what everyone brings to a Christening then! Couldn't you have got him a rattle or something? Could have been a gold-plated rattle, or diamond encrusted if you need to be a bit flash. No? Oh well. Anyway, leave your pressies and get out of here. Quick! And sneak back to… er… wherever that place is where wise men live in the East. All right?

Melchior – So no saying toodle pip to Herod then?

Gabriel – No! No saying anything to Hagrid! Not at all. Don't even wave as you go past.

Melchior – Shame. He's got the biggest widescreen TV I've ever seen…

Gabriel – Yea, and you and your mates'll be on it in the news about three missing wise men buried in concrete overcoats, if you drop in on Mr Wormy-guts. Go home! And quick. Now, how do I get out of your dream? I think I have to squeeze back through your ear like this…

Melchior – Ow!!

Gabriel – Sorry! No easy way I'm afraid. Bye.

Gabriel wanders off.

Eight

Gabriel is resting up in heaven now, his work done, supping a supersize glass of milk and honey.

Michael – Gabe! What are you doing back here?

Gabriel – What? I did the job. I told the wise men, they're packing up their camels and heading for the sunset even as we speak. I told them King Hagrid's got the smelly lurgy, so they won't go near him.

Michael – But what about Joseph?

Gabriel – He hasn't got the lurgy. He smelt fine the last time I saw him.

Michael – No! Why aren't you down there invading his dream and telling him to pack up his troubles and head for the sun?

Gabriel – The sun?

Michael – Egypt!

Gabriel – Ooh I've always wanted to go to Egypt, they've got these really ancient huge…

Michael – Get down there now! Quick! Before that putrefying Herod pitches up with a hundred sword-bearing no-goods. We've got to get them out of there. Go! Now!

Gabriel – All right, but could you put my supersize milk and honey in the fridge, I hate it when it gets all tepid…

Michael – Go!

Gabriel hurries off. Michael sniffs the milk and honey and takes a sip. He nods happily to himself and wanders off with it.

Nine

So Gabriel goes, and finds Joseph asleep next to Mary and their baby boy. It takes a little while for Gabriel to squeeze under his pillow and down past Joe's eardrum as he is wearing particularly snug earplugs because he's not been sleeping too well with Jesus waking up for a feed every couple of hours. But Gabriel gets in there in the end.

Gabriel – Psst! Pssssssssssst! Joe. Oy! It's me.

Joseph – What… where… where am I?

Gabriel – Actually back at school. It's one of those dreams where you're walking round and round and you can't find the right classroom, you know the ones?

Joseph – Oh no! I hate those.

Gabriel – Don't worry, it's really so I can have a chat with you.

Joseph – Not another one! Who's pregnant now?

Gabriel – Nobody! Don't panic. Well - do panic actually. Hagrid's about to kill you.

Joseph – WHAT!! But I'm stuck in school and I can't find the way out!!

Gabriel – It's all right. Hagrid's not coming here to your old school. He'd only get lost in all the corridors anyway. He'd be wandering around aimlessly trying to find the right room for his GCSE exam in annihilation. So there's no need to panic, as soon as you wake up, you'll be home again and everything'll be all right. Well, when I say all right what I mean of course is 'all right' apart from Hagrid coming with a hundred soldiers to wipe you and everybody else out.

Joseph – Does Mary know?

Gabriel – Not yet. But she will soon.

Joseph – Is that your next job?

Gabriel – No it's yours.

Joseph – What??

Gabriel – Yea, you need to break it to her that a bunch of sweaty, cut-throat yobs are coming to get you. You might want to do it gently. Give her some flowers or something. You could put it on a little card in a box of chocolates.

Joseph – How come I have to tell her that Herod's gonna kill us? Why can't you? You were quite happy to pitch up in our kitchen and tell her she was pregnant. How come I get the horrible job?

Gabriel – Actually I told her in the street. And it was quite a nerve-racking job. She was carrying two rather dangerous-looking shopping bags. She might have hit me with a box of eggs. And it wasn't a box of 6, there were 12 in there. Large size as well, d'you know what I mean?

Joseph – This is terrible. First we have to cancel the big wedding because of the embarrassment about her being pregnant, then we have to up and run away from home when she's about to give birth so I can come to Bethlehem for the census. Then a bunch of shepherds turn up stinking of sheep poo and now I have to tell her it's all for nothing.

Gabriel – Actually you missed the bit about the weird wise men pitching up with gold, Frankenstein and myrrh. I mean, why they couldn't have just bought a rattle and a book token I don't know… and anyway, it's not all for nothing. This is the biggest assignment in history. You'll be all right. Honest.

Joseph – You mean we don't have to run for our lives?

Gabriel – Oh I didn't say that. How can I put this…? Basically… yes, you do have to run for your lives. Pretty quickly actually. In fact you're making this dream a lot longer than it needs to be. And I've already had a busy night. I had to tell the wise men to scarper too.

Joseph – Are they in trouble as well?

Gabriel – I'll say. They should never have gone to see old Wormy-guts, they really need to get a Sat Nav.

Joseph – A what?

Gabriel – Don't worry, you're not outside of time like me. Anyway, grab Mary and the baby, and pack a few things. Don't forget the gold and the Frankenstein… especially the gold, that'll help you finance the trip - you know, pay for a nice place with a good view and en suite down in Egypt.

Joseph – In Egypt!

Gabriel – Yea, you could see the Pyramids while you're there! And the Sphinx. Bring back a fridge magnet or two. Now hurry up, I'm off and don't worry about wandering the corridors here and being trapped in your old school dream, any minute now you'll go through the next door and wake up and be home, just follow this corridor here… oh… hang on, which way do we go? Oh no! I think I'm trapped in your old school dream now. And isn't it time for my English Literature GCSE?

I feel totally unprepared! How do I get out! Help! Agh!!

Somehow they both manage to get out of the dream.

Ten

Gabriel sighs and puffs out his cheeks as he wanders back to heaven. He talks as he goes.

Gabriel – It's hard work being an angel. It's not all wings and halos. In fact we don't have wings. It's a myth you know.

Michael appears and walks up to him.

Michael – Why are you talking to yourself Gabe?

Gabriel – What? Me? No I'm talking to the reader. They think angels have wings.

Michael – Really? Wings, eh? That would be fun. Anyway, how did the dream go?

Gabriel – Well I got trapped in Joseph's old school. Couldn't find the right room for my English Literature exam. Took me three hours to find the way out.

Michael – Yes but what about Mary and Joseph? Are they safe?

Gabriel – I think so. I told them to go to Egypt.

Michael – Good. Well done. Because Herod's on the way right now. It's gonna be terrible.

Gabriel – Couldn't I go down and warn everyone? Couldn't we send a squad of angels to fight the bad guys?

Michael – I'd love to Gabe, but it's not allowed. I don't know why, I don't have the big picture, I just know a few bits and pieces. I'm terrified something disastrous might happen to the baby. How will he survive and be okay on a planet like earth? It's mad down there at times. That's why he's gone down there, you know.

Gabriel – What do you mean?

Michael – That's what this is all about. Sorting out the mess.

Gabriel – The boss should just send another flood, wipe out all the silliness down there all over again.

Michael – Can't, have you never seen the rainbows?

Gabriel – The rainbows?

Michael – Yes. They're a reminder for him, he's promised to do things another way. That's what this is about. Changing things. But with less water and more humans.

Gabriel – Humans? Bit of a risk if you ask me. Have you seen that lot down there? Some of them couldn't organise an omelette in an egg-packing factory. What's his plan b?

Michael – No plan b. Just changing things one person at a time.

Gabriel – Not very *X Factor* is it? Not very *'summer blockbustery.'* I mean, it all seems a bit low key. That won't set Twitter on fire.

Michael – Totally. Now, listen, you've got a day off tomorrow, but the next day we want you back down there breaking into Joseph's dreams again.

Gabriel – So soon? But they won't have seen the Pyramids.

Michael – What? Listen, time in heaven is not like time there. By the time you've put your feet up and watched a few box sets Herod's gonna be dead and it'll be time for Mary and Joseph to come home.

Gabriel – Ooh box sets! I love box sets. Have I got time to watch the whole of *The Vicar of Dibley*, *Rev* <u>and</u> *Father Ted*?

Michael – No idea. Off you go…

Eleven

Somewhere in Egypt. Some time at night. Somewhere under Joseph's pillow.

Gabriel – Right, here we go again, under the pillow, past the earplug... ouch! Squeeze squeeze squee-e-e-e-e-e-e-eze... and we're in. Now where is he? Aha. Psst! Joe! Psst!

Joseph – What? Not you again! Oh no! Not another lost-in-the-corridors school dream. What now? Mary's not expecting again, is she?

Gabriel – No! It's Herod.

Joseph – Herod's expecting?!

Gabriel – No. He's dead.

Joseph – What!

Gabriel – You heard. He's gone. Snuffed it. He is no more. Ceased to be. Bereft of life he rests in peace. He's an ex-Herod. He's shuffled off this mortal coil and is pushing up the daisies. Have you never seen Monty Python?

Joseph – Monty who?

Gabriel – Dead Parrot sketch.

Joseph – Dead what? Parrot? Did Herod kill him then?

Gabriel – No. He wasn't very well.

Joseph – Who? Herod or the parrot?

Gabriel – Both actually. Herod was in a terrible state. Lots of his bits were dropping off at the end. He went loopy too. Still, couldn't have happened to a nicer guy! Never mind that though. The point is – he's gone. You're safe.

Joseph – Are you sure?

Gabriel – Well, no I didn't check his pulse, and I didn't get to the funeral. Knowing Herod I doubt if there were many angels there really. But I have it on good authority. The best authority. Did you see the Pyramids by the way? Awesome eh? D'you get some nice fridge magnets?

Joseph – Where are we supposed to go now?

Gabriel – Back home. Back to Israel. Start bringing up this beautiful baby of yours. Get him ready for a trip to the temple when he's 12, so that you can forget to bring him home and panic about where he is, have to go running back… and then ground him for 18 years till he's 30.

Joseph – What?

Gabriel – Only kidding. Well I'm not actually, some of that will happen, but you needn't worry at the moment. You'll have plenty to do watching him turn into a toddler, falling over and messing about with the other boys, playing and scraping his knees and eating worms. All those happy childhood things. Now don't forget to pack everything. The gold and what-not.

Joseph – We spent most of the gold. We've still got the myrrh though.

Gabriel – Oh great! The ominous gift. Oh well... How's Mary?

Joseph – All right. She's been through a lot though. It's not been easy.

Gabriel – No. And just wait till he grows up. My goodness, all the stuff that's round the corner...

Joseph – What?

Gabriel – Oh don't worry. Just love one another and take care of each other and you'll be fine. Happy Christmas by the way.

Joseph – Happy what?

Gabriel – It's what people will say in years to come. When they celebrate at this time of year.

Joseph – You mean they'll remember us?

Gabriel – Sort of... a lot of people will just panic about whether they've got a big enough turkey and plenty of chocolates for the tree, but some folks will remember. And they'll talk a lot about you. They'll sing songs and tell each other stories about what happened. About your courage and the census and you taking Mary to Bethlehem. You're changing the world you know?

Joseph – Really? Wow! How?

Gabriel – Little by little. Minute by minute. When your boy grows up…

Joseph – What? Will he be powerful and famous? Will he be king?

Gabriel – Yes. Sort of.

Joseph – With lots of servants and a big palace?

Gabriel – Not exactly.

Joseph – He'll have a good long life though?

Gabriel – Er… well, that's the problem with changing the world. He'll have to fight some battles.

Joseph – He's going to be a soldier?

Gabriel – No. Not those kind of battles. It won't be easy for him. And ultimately it'll look like he's lost. And then unexpectedly everything will change and look different. And life will never be the same.

Joseph – Will he have a big palace after that?

Gabriel – Not really. It's complicated. But you're a vital part of it. I'd best go. It's the Inter-angelic FA Cup Final. Cherubim Wednesday are playing.

Joseph – Can I come? I could just do with a bit of time out now.

Gabriel – I'm afraid not. You need to get on and bring up your son. Like I said - vital job that. Really important. You're a world-changer Joe. It's always about the little things you know, they might seem ordinary, and not very *'summer blockbustery'*, but they're vital. Keep going, don't give up… bye then.

Gabriel smiles at Joseph, shakes his hand and leaves. Joseph looks thoughtful as he walks off in the wrong direction, then realises he's going the wrong way, turns and hurries off in the other direction.

Printed in Great Britain
by Amazon